www.frontiercollege.ca
This book is brought to you by
Frontier College
and our generous supporters

FRONTIER
COLLEGE

COLLÈGE
FRONTIÈRE

Ce livre vous est gracieusement
présenté par Collège Frontière
et ses généréux donateurs

www.collegefrontiere.ca

Special Effects

SCHOLASTIC

SYDNEY AUCKLAND NEW YORK TORONTO LONDON MEXICO CITY
NEW DELHI HONG KONG BUENOS AIRES PUERTO RICO

Enter the X·Zone!

Every **X·Zone** book is full of facts and amazing true stories that will take you around the world and back.

You'll find vivid photos and illustrations that will spark your imagination.

One thing to keep in mind: If you see a word in **bold**, look in the glossary for the meaning!

Ready for an adventure in reading?

Then enter the **X·Zone!**

Lights, camera, action!

Contents

Did this really happen?

PAGE **4**

Why did ET have such a long neck?

PAGE **13**

Can ancient giants really come to life?

PAGE **20**

SPECIAL EFFECTS MOVIE MAGIC

I've made a flip book for you! I changed my drawing on each page, just like frames of a film.

It's hard to imagine a world without movies and movie special effects. SPFX (as special effects are known) make the impossible appear possible. When the lights dim and the music plays, audiences know that anything can happen! Monsters and aliens become real. Superman can fly. Dinosaurs and gladiators can come back to life.

Moving Pictures

Before 1895, no-one had heard of movies or movie SPFX. People were used to still black-and-white photographs, but moving pictures were just a dream.

In the 1890s, French brothers Antoine and Louis Lumiere developed a machine called the *cinematograph*. This amazing machine could record and project moving images.

The first-ever movie was shown in Paris in 1895. Ten black-and-white films were shown, none more than a minute in length. But the crowd was delighted. People jumped from their seats in fright when a train rushed on screen. They were worried that it might run them over! It all seemed so real.

On that night in Paris, movie magic was born.

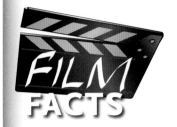

FILM FACTS

Only 33 people bought tickets for the Lumieres' first movie screening. Today, movie premieres can earn millions of dollars.

The *First Special Effects Wizard*

George Melies was the first SPFX wizard. He started his career as a stage magician.

George had seen the Lumiere brothers' first demonstration of the cinematograph. He was amazed to see their moving pictures.

This inspired him to use the tricks he had learned as a stage magician to make the first SPFX movies. In 1897 he produced his first movie, *Voyage to the Moon*. It was the very first SPFX **blockbuster**. In the movie, a team of explorers were shot to the moon using a giant cannon. They were captured, and imprisoned by evil moon creatures. Eventually they defeated the aliens and returned to Earth.

The whole movie was only 13 minutes long. George Melies used stage tricks, mirrors, and basic lighting effects to create his **sci-fi** thriller.

My octopus is looking good. What would you draw for your flick book?

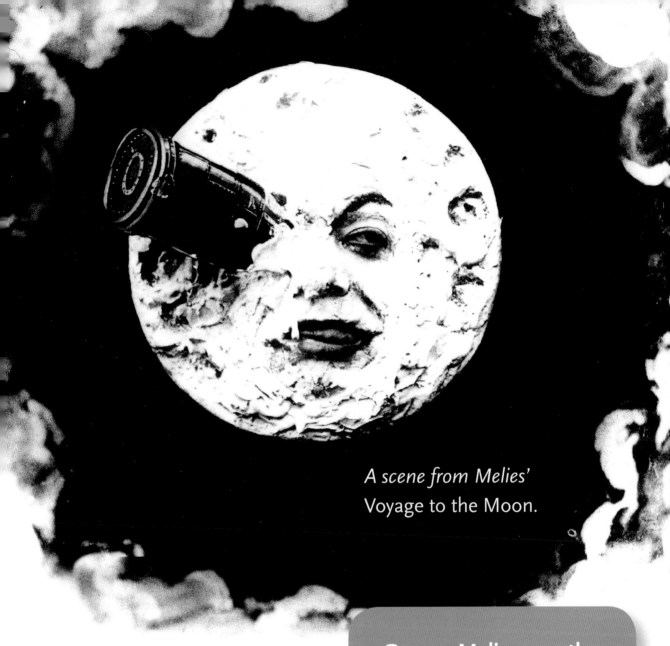

A scene from Melies' Voyage to the Moon.

George Melies became famous for his SPFX movies. His movie *Voyage Beyond the Possible* was about explorers heading to the sun! Other movies by this early movie maker were 20,000 *Leagues Under the Sea, Journey into Space,* and *The Conquest of the Pole.*

George Melies was the first true SPFX wizard. His movies were black-and-white and silent. But they captured people's imagination. In his movies anything seemed possible.

UNLEASHING MONSTERS

During the 1950s and 1960s, SPFX movies became very popular. By now colour and sound had been invented. In this era, science-fiction movies were usually about humans versus UFOS, alien invaders, and hideous monsters.

Watching *The War of the Worlds* (about Martians invading the Earth, and based on the book by H G Wells) today, we might laugh at the strings we can see holding up the Martian spacecraft. But in 1953, movies like this were considered very scary!

Stop-motion Marvels

Filmmaker, Ray Harryhausen, also loved tales of wonder. He saw movies as a place for fantasy, not real life. He used a technique called **stop-motion** animation.

Unlike today's computer animators, Harryhausen had to build his creatures. In 1955 he made the movie *It Came From Beneath the Sea*, where a giant octopus was supposed to attack San Francisco. This was where he used stop-motion animation.

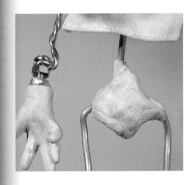

A stop-motion model has a skeleton just like you.

How Does Stop-motion Work?

First, Harryhausen made a model of the octopus. Thanks to its metal skeleton, the model could be shaped into any pose.

Then for each **frame** of film, Harryhausen moved the octopus slightly. A frame is like a still photograph.

When played together, the slight changes in each frame combined into a continuous moving picture of the octopus.

Stop motion was a slow and expensive process. Just a few minutes of stop-motion animation took months to film, but the finished result was spectacular. Monsters came to life!

Harryhausen in his studio.

In his film *Jason and the Argonauts*, Harryhausen used stop-motion to create an army of skeletons. You can imagine the hard work and time involved in creating that army.

In the modern movie *Pirates of the Caribbean*, computers were used to bring skeletons to life in a similar scene.

Harryhausen's stop-motion skeletons were special for their time. They are a high point in SPFX history. Films like *Chicken Run* use the same stop-motion methods today.

CREATURE FEATURES

Directors George Lucas and Steven Spielberg combined great storytelling with state-of-the-art SPFX. They transformed modern movie making.

Between them, Lucas and Spielberg have created some of the best-loved movies of all time.

The *Terrible Sinking* **Shark**

In 1975, Steven Spielberg directed the movie *Jaws*, a movie about a killer shark. He knew that special effects would be needed to create the shark because a real shark would have been impossible to control. The computers SPFX artists use today weren't around when *Jaws* was shot, so the shark had to be built. Almost everybody told Spielberg that this was impossible. It nearly was.

Spielberg and Jaws

Jaws *was Steven Spielberg's second movie. He went on to make many of the most popular movies of all time—including* Close Encounters of the Third Kind, Raiders of the Lost Ark, Jurassic Park, *and* E.T.

Almost all of Spielberg's films feature special effects.

Using a technique called **animatronics**, Spielberg's SPFX team built a full-scale shark. It was a large robotic puppet operated by remote control. The shark was built with a steel skeleton, a latex skin and pneumatics (air-operated mechanisms) which controlled its movements.

Quiet on the set! Action!

JAWS

CREATURE FEATURES
Salt Water Worries

For one scene, Spielberg wanted the shark to be pulled through the water. Everything was going according to plan until the shark sank to the bottom of the sea, and divers were called to recover it! Saltwater had gotten into the shark, and it kept breaking down. The actors spent hours waiting around for the shark to be repaired, but it never really worked perfectly.

The shark was hardly scary. It was an SPFX disaster. But the actors' patience—and some careful **editing**—paid off.

Good actors, a clever script, and careful direction ensured that *Jaws* became one of the biggest movie hits of all time. And that leaky, sinking shark became one of the scariest creatures in SPFX history.

More Than
Just Scary

Like many SPFX movies, *Jaws* was intended to scare people. Since the days of *King Kong* back in 1932, almost all SPFX movies were action films. But Steven Spielberg wanted to prove that SPFX could do more than just make movies scary.

E.T. The Extraterrestrial is the story of a friendship between a human boy and an alien creature. Using animatronics, Spielberg created a creature with realistic facial expressions and emotions. The E.T. puppet was operated from off-screen by a team of puppeteers.

> Spielberg gave E.T. a long neck so that no-one would think he was just a person dressed up in a suit.

FILM FACTS

In an interview about the movie, Drew Barrymore, one of the stars, said, "E.T. was absolutely real to me." And audiences seemed to agree. People fell in love with E.T. He made them laugh and cry. No-one ever thought of E.T as just a special effect. He always seemed real.

SPFX *Wars*

George Lucas' *Star Wars* movies are the most popular SPFX movies of all time. We all know the story of Luke Skywalker and his fight against Darth Vader and the Empire.

In 1977, George Lucas first brought his story of that galaxy, far, far away to life. He gathered together the finest SPFX artists of the day. Lucas created a team called *Industrial Light and Magic*, or ILM for short.

ILM is still the world's leading SPFX organization.

Using a combination of stop-motion, puppetry, models, and full-scale costumes and sets, ILM brought *Star Wars* to life.

George Lucas used every trick in the book to make *Star Wars* seem real.

To become an alien like Chewbacca or Greedo, an actor must wear SPFX makeup and **prosthetics**. A prosthetic is attached to the actor's body, like extra arms, or horns on the head. Prosthetics can make an actor look hurt and scarred, like Darth Vader without his helmet in *The Return of the Jedi,* or incredibly wrinkled, like the Emperor, below.

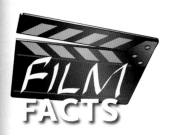

FILM FACTS

Did you know that Jabba the Hutt's Rancor beast in Return of the Jedi *was stop-motion? Or that Yoda (below) in* The Empire Strikes Back *was a hand puppet, operated by puppeteer Frank Oz. He also created Miss Piggy from* The Muppets.

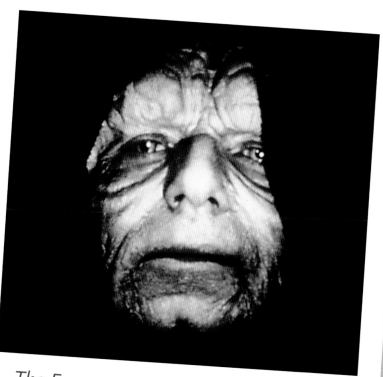

The Emperor, The Empire Strikes Back

Directors, Stephen Spielberg and George Lucas showed us that SPFX could make people laugh and cry as well as they could frighten and surprise.

DIGITAL MAGIC

The 1990s saw a massive boom in the number of SPFX movies. Before this time all SPFX had to be physically built. But computers, with their digital magic, would change SPFX forever.

Two movies in particular were among the first to use these amazing new techniques.

Metal Men

In *Terminator 2: Judgment Day*, director James Cameron brought back the characters of his 1984 movie, *The Terminator*.

But now there was new computer technology that hadn't been available when the first *Terminator* movie was made. The SPFX teams had to decide which effects could be achieved physically, and which had to be done by computer.

The most incredible SPFX in *Terminator 2* were used to bring the evil T-1000 to life. Played by actor Robert Patrick, the T-1000 could heal itself when injured, turn its arms into weapons, and change its shape to seem like someone else. Only a computer could create these amazing effects. Computer-generated images, (or **CGI**), allowed animators to bring the T-1000 to life.

Director, James Cameron, with Arnold Schwarzenegger.

In the case of the T-1000, only computers could create its amazing abilities. With the help of new computer technology, Cameron created a SPFX blockbuster. It started a new and exciting era in SPFX.

FILM FACTS

Almost 16 minutes of Terminator 2 is entirely SPFX!

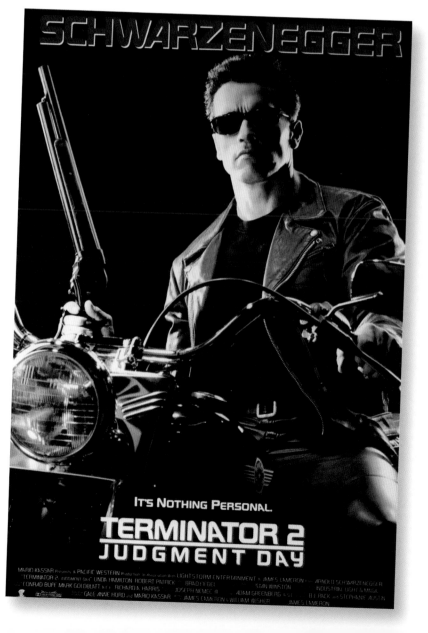

SCHWARZENEGGER

IT'S NOTHING PERSONAL.

TERMINATOR 2
JUDGMENT DAY

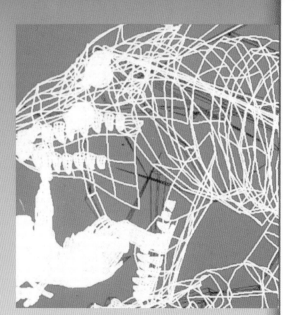

The first step is to map a model of the character and create a grid using a computer.

This grid provides the basis for the final, realistic computer-generated image.

How Were the T-1000 Effects Created?

To give the T-1000 its incredible powers, SPFX artists had to create a computerised model of Patrick's body. They painted a grid on his body and filmed him walking. The points on the grid showed the artists how Patrick's muscles and bones moved when he walked. This information was entered into a computer.

Now the artists had a very believable computerised Patrick look-alike. They could make him do anything they wanted, like change shape, walk through fire, and survive thousands of gunshots unharmed!

To create realistic close-up shots of the T-1000's face, the artists had to create a three-dimensional computerised model of Patrick's face. To do this, they used a laser to scan his face into a computer.

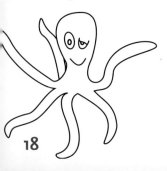

18

The incredible liquid metal and **morphing** effects used in Terminator 2 *have become a favourite of SPFX wizards and audiences. Morphing involves the changing of one object into another.*

Can you believe 15 seconds of film took nearly eight weeks to make?

Bringing *the* **Past** *to* **Life**

One of the biggest hits of the 1990s was *Jurassic Park*.

Directed by Steven Spielberg, this SPFX-driven movie brought dinosaurs stunningly back to life.

Spielberg was a big fan of Ray Harryhausen. He had planned to use stop-motion to create the dinosaurs of *Jurassic Park*.

But *Terminator 2* changed everything. It proved that computer technology was ready to tackle any SPFX challenge.

Spielberg decided to use computer-generated images for his movie instead.

Because there are no dinosaurs alive today, CGI animators studied the movements of living reptiles.

The animators worked with dinosaur experts, learning everything they could about dinosaurs. The SPFX artists made models of each dinosaur, designing every detail— even their skin. *Jurassic Park's* dinosaurs had to seem like living animals.

Some of the *Jurassic Park* dinosaurs were created physically, like the large animatronic T-Rex.

Like working with the shark in *Jaws*, working with the animatronic T-Rex was difficult. In the movie, the major T-Rex attack occured in the rain. During the filming of the scene the dinosaur soaked up water, and became very heavy. It needed constant drying down.

In spite of the difficulties filming, *Jurassic Park* was a monster of a success.

Today we are used to seeing CGI monsters at the movies. But without *Jurassic Park*, dinosaurs might still be extinct, even in the movies!

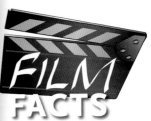

FILM FACTS

The Jurassic Park animators took classes to practise walking like dinosaurs! This helped them get a feel for how a dinosaur should move.

This is harder than it looks!

Using technology from *Terminator 2* and *Jurassic Park*, many amazing SPFX movies appeared during the late 1990s.

The Matrix *Unloads*

With their high kicks, somersaults and incredible acrobatics, actors Keanu Reeves and Carrie-Anne Moss certainly looked cool in *The Matrix*.

From the opening scene, audiences knew that the movie's creators, Andy and Larry Wachowski had made a sci-fi film like no other.

The Wachowski brothers were fans of comic books, and Japanese animation, and wanted a whole new look for their movie. They created a new special effect called **bullet-time** *photography*.

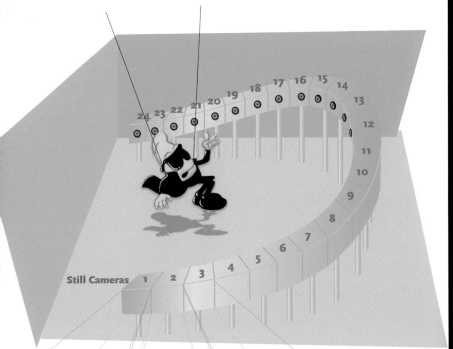

Each still photograph becomes a frame in the film. The slightly different angle in each frame creates the feeling of movement.

How Does Bullet-Time Photography Work?

First, a large number of still cameras, **1–24**, are placed around the actor. Then the actor, held in place by wires, launches into action.

At the exact same moment, each camera takes a still photograph of the actor. These individual photographs are joined together as frames in the film.

Because each frame shows the actor from a slightly different angle, the film looks like a single camera has spun around the actor, frozen in time. This is as high-tech as SPFX can get!

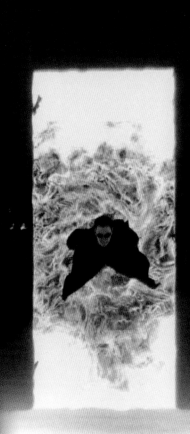

Keanu Reeves can fly through the air by the magic of SPFX.

Return to the *Galaxy* Far, Far, Away

Screens coloured blue and green are used because these colours are not found in actors' skin tones.

In 1999, more than 20 years after the first *Star Wars* movie, George Lucas released *Star Wars: Episode One— The Phantom Menace.*

Many of the same SPFX artists who worked on the 1977 original returned. But this time teams of digital animators were used.

Computers were also used to create creatures and landscapes. Twenty years ago they had to be built by hand.

Computers were used to create creatures and landscapes that 20 years ago would have been created by hand.

The actors often appeared in locations that did not exist outside the computer.

So, how did this work?

The actors performed in front of empty screens painted green or blue. Digital SPFX artists later filled these empty spaces with fabulous detail. And presto—the actors appeared to be on the planets of Tatooine, Naboo, and Coruscant!

One of the most unusual new additions to the *Star Wars* universe was Jar Jar Binks. He was the first ever fully CGI character to star in a movie.

The animators had to make sure that Jar Jar blended in with his human co-stars. Jar Jar's skin and clothing had to seem as real as the actor Ewan McGregor's.

A scene using a blue screen which will later be replaced by computer-generated effects.

Some of the effects are real, such as water spray and the boat's movement.

The completed scene looks totally real.

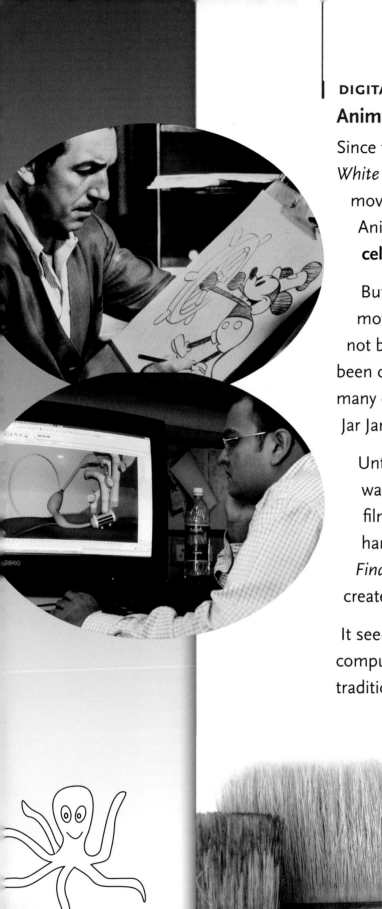

Animation: Paint or Computer?

Since the days of Walt Disney's *Snow White and the Seven Dwarfs*, animated movies have been mostly hand-drawn. Animators painted the thousands of **cels** needed to bring a story to life.

But in the last few years, animated movies like *Toy Story* and *Shrek* have not been drawn by hand. They have been created using a computer, using many of the same tricks needed to bring Jar Jar to life.

Until recently, Disney's *The Lion King* was the most successful animated film of all time. It was created using hand-drawn cels. But in 2003, *Finding Nemo* took the record. It was created using a computer.

It seems that audiences now prefer computer-animated movies to traditional cel animation.

What Does the Future Hold?

A synthespian from Final Fantasy: The Spirits Within

Today, stories can be brought to life in ways that George Melies could only have dreamt of.

If a writer can dream up a T-Rex or a Terminator, then a SPFX wizard can bring them to life.

The human characters in *Final Fantasy: The Spirits Within* were entirely computer-generated, but they seem very real.

This level of realism leads many people to wonder whether *synthespians* (actors created entirely by computer) will replace real, live actors. Could actors from the past come back in computerised form? Will there be a new category at the Oscars® for synthespians?

There is no telling what the future holds for special effects. As computers become more powerful and directors more creative, it seems that anything is possible—but only in the movies.

Quiz

1. The cinematograph was a device designed to record and project moving pictures. It was developed by
   a) the Wachowski Brothers
   b) George Melies
   c) the Lumiere Brothers
   d) Ray Harryhausen

2. Which of these directors began his career as a stage magician?
   a) George Lucas
   b) Steven Spielberg
   c) Andy Wachowski
   d) George Melies

3. Ray Harryhausen was a pioneer of which SPFX technique?
   a) stop-motion animation
   b) CGI
   c) animatronics
   d) bullet-time photography

4. A full sized animatronic shark was built for which movie?
   a) *20,000 Leagues Under the Sea*
   b) *The Empire Strikes Back*
   c) *Jaws*
   d) *Jurassic Park*

5. Synthespians are actors created entirely by a computer.
   True/False?

6. Extra ears, legs, or arms attached to an actor are called
   a) prosthetics
   b) animatronics
   c) morphs
   d) animatics

7. In *Terminator 2* which technique was used to change one object into another?
   a) blue screen
   b) motion capture
   c) stop-motion
   d) morphing

8. The first fully CGI lead character in movie history was
   a) Gollum
   b) Jaws
   c) King Kong
   d) Jar Jar Binks

9. Bullet-time photography was developed for which movie?
   a) *Jason and the Argonauts*
   b) *The Matrix*
   c) *Voyage to the Moon*
   d) *Star Wars: Episode Two*

10. George Lucas' SPFX company is called
   a) Lumiere Productions
   b) Weta Workshop
   c) Industrial Light and Magic
   d) Yoda's Box of Tricks

Answers

10 c)
9 b)
8 d)
7 d)
6 a)
5 True
4 c)
3 a)
2 d)
1 c)

28

Glossary

animatronics Complex robotic puppets operated by puppeteers.

blockbuster A large, expensive production that is expected to make a lot of money at the box office.

bullet-time Technique made famous by *The Matrix*. A circle of cameras photographs an actor, creating the impression of frozen time.

cels Single images used to create hand-drawn animation.

CGI Computer-generated images. These are SPFX created entirely using a computer.

editing Choosing and assembling the best scenes and shots from many hours of raw film.

frame A still moment of film. There are 24 frames per second in a film.

morphing The art of transforming one object into another object using CGI.

prosthetics A makeup appliance attached to an actor to create an unusual effect.

sci-fi (science fiction) A made-up story based on scientific knowledge.

stop-motion Technique made famous by Ray Harryhausen. This frame-by-frame animation makes models appear to move.

Index